THE TEN COMMANDMENTS for Children

H.J. Richards

THE LITURGICAL PRESS
Collegeville, Minnesota 56321

McCRIMMON'S
Great Wakering Essex

First published in Great Britain in 1988 by
McCRIMMON PUBLISHING CO LTD
10-12 High Street, Great Wakering, Essex

McCrimmons ISBN 0 85597 408 7
Liturgical Press ISBN 0–8146–1801–4

Photo credits:
Cover Photo by John Fisher
p.3 George W. Allan
p.4 UNRWA photo
p.5 Barnaby's Picture Library
p.6 Barnaby's Picture Library
p.8 Barnaby's Picture Library
p.10 Eastern Daily Press
p.12 Eastern Daily Press
p.14 Popperfoto
p.16 UNRWA photo by G. Nehmeh
p.18 Syndication International
p.20 Eastern Daily Press
p.22 Eastern Daily Press
p.24 Popperfoto
p.26 Photo by John Fisher
p.28 UNRWA photo

Cover design by Paul Shuttleworth
Typesetting by Barry Sarling, Rayleigh, Essex
Printed by Mayhew McCrimmon Printers Ltd
Great Wakering, Essex

INTRODUCTION

The **Ten Commandments** are the ten basic rules which our ancestors agreed to live by, more than three thousand years ago.

They received them from their leader, Moses.

He said, 'This is how God wants you to live.'

All people, everywhere, have always admired these rules. They have the ring of truth about them, like Maker's Instructions. Jesus himself obeyed them, and taught them.

The **Ten Commandments** begin with the words:
'I am the God who rescued you from slavery.
Therefore... (1,2,3,4,5,6,7,8,9,10).'

This can be understood in two ways.

It could mean:

1. 'I rescued you from one slavemaster.
   Now you are *my* slaves.
   These are my rules.'

Or it could mean:

2. 'I saw you when you were slaves
   and had pity on you.
   I took your side and decided
   to set you free.
   Now you are my people,
   specially dear to me.
   I will teach you how to live
   happily.
   When you've learnt, you can go
   and teach other people.

This second way is how we Jews and Christians have always understood the **Ten Commandments**.

This does not mean that the Commandments are like a competition, for which we shall be rewarded if we do well.

God doesn't love us because *we* are good, but because *he* is good.

The Commandments are more like signposts put up by God, to tell us whether we are on the right path, or off it.

Put God first

i. Thou shalt not have strange gods before me.

1. PUT GOD FIRST, BEFORE ANYONE OR ANYTHING ELSE.

What do we put first?
Looking after ourselves without thinking of others?
That is making ourselves into God.
Collecting lots of good things for ourselves?
That is making things into our God.
Having power over people in order to boss them about?
That is making power into our God.

The first Commandment says our life will be miserable if we don't give our whole heart and mind to the real God.

A psalmist sang:

I say to the Lord, 'You are my God,
My happiness lies in you alone.' *(Psalm 16:2)*

God is mysterious

ii. Thou shalt not make to thyself any graven thing.

2. *REALISE THAT GOD IS GREATER THAN ANY IDEA YOU HAVE OF HIM.*

God is mysterious.
Our minds are too small to understand him.
What we *do* understand is always something less than he is himself.
God is always greater than our ideas of him.
We must worship God himself, not our small ideas of him.

A prophet asked:

To whom can you compare God?
There is no one.
What image can show you what he is really like?
There is none. *(Isaiah 40:25)*

Make sure God approves

iii. Thou shalt not take the name of the Lord thy God in vain.

3. USE THE WORD 'GOD' SPARINGLY.

The word 'God' means less and less the more we use it:
'O God', 'I hope to God',
'God's truth', 'God help us',
'God knows', 'Thank God',
'God forbid', 'For God's sake',
'Good God', 'God says'.

We shouldn't use the word when we don't need to.
And if we need to say we are doing something in God's name,
we should make sure he approves.

Jesus said:

It is not people who keep on saying, 'Lord, Lord',
who will enter the Kingdom of God,
but those who do the will of my Father in heaven.
(Matthew 7:21)

No time off

iv. Remember that thou keep holy the Sabbath day.

4. REMIND YOURSELF THAT GOD IS WITH YOU EVERY DAY.

Show respect to God by stopping from time to time to be aware of him standing by you.
Some people are never given a chance to do so: they have to work too hard.
This Commandment tells those in charge of people to give them time off.
People are not to be turned into machines.

In one of the psalms, God is heard saying:

Be still and know that I am God. *(Psalm 46:10)*

The brother or sister you can see

The first four Commandments have to do with loving God.
The last six have to do with loving our neighbours.
Because the only way we have of telling whether we really love God is the way we treat other people.

St John said:

Anyone who says, 'I love God',
and doesn't love his brother or sister,
is telling lies.
If you don't love the brother or sister
whom you can see,
you can't say you're loving the God
whom you can't see. *(1 John 5:20)*

They gave life to you

v. Honour thy father and thy mother.

5. *LOVE YOUR NEIGHBOURS BY RESPECTING YOUR PARENTS.*

They gave life to you.
Be grateful, and give life to them.
We should respect also all the other people who give life to us:
our relatives
our teachers
people who help us
people who are in charge.

St Paul said:

Children, be obedient to your parents always.
That is what God wants.
Parents, do not irritate your children,
or they will lose heart.
Everyone, be obedient to those who are in charge,
even when they're not watching you: God is.
Those who are in charge, treat people fairly:
God is watching you too. *(Colossians 3:20 - 4:1)*

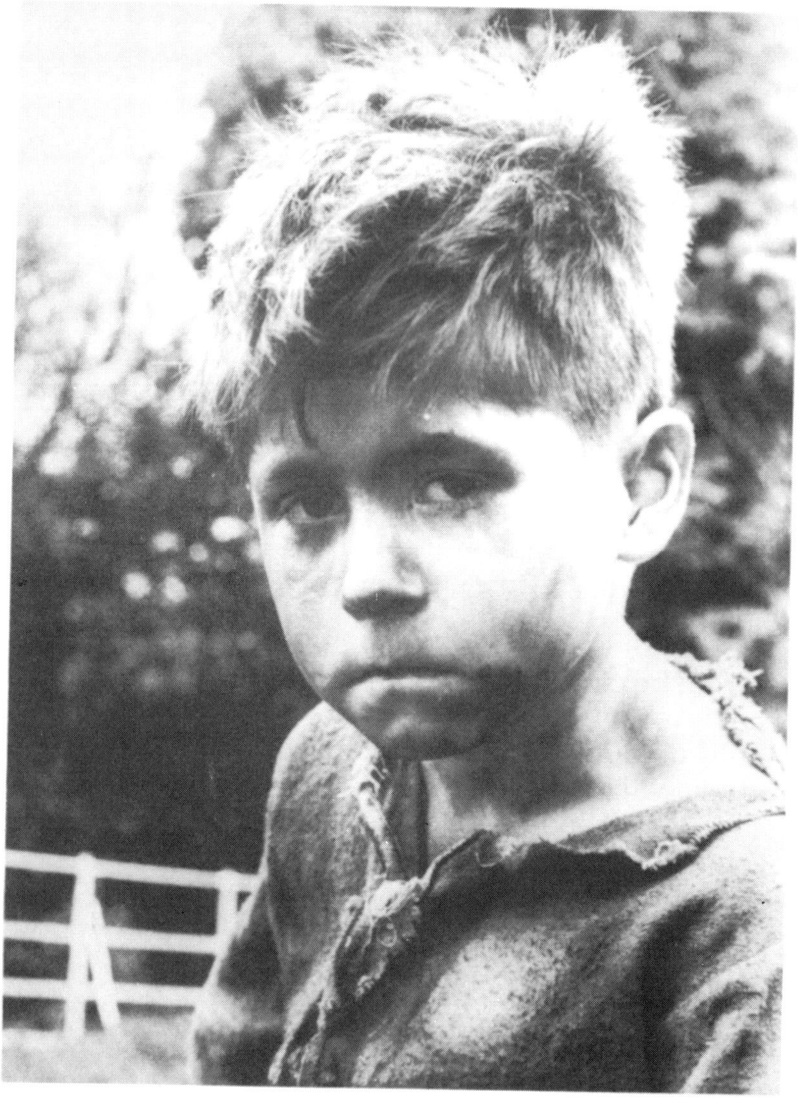

Not even in the things you think

vi. Thou shalt not kill.

6. *LOVE YOUR NEIGHBOURS BY NEVER DOING THEM ANY HARM.*

Not even in the things you say.
Not even in the things you think.
No grudges or bad temper.
No spitefulness.
No hatred or revenge.
Not even against those who don't love you:
God loves them.
Be helpful and gentle with everyone.
Make peace, not war.

Jesus said:

You must set no limits to your love,
just as God sets none to his. *(Matthew 5:48)*

Staying friends

vii. Thou shalt not commit adultery.

7. LOVE YOUR NEIGHBOUR BY STAYING FRIENDS WITH THE PERSON YOU MARRY.

Marrying is still a long way away for you.
But it's worth thinking now about staying friends with people.
Sharing with them.
Putting yourself out for them.
Forgiving them.
Asking them to forgive you.
If we can't stay friends with people now,
we'll find it hard to stay friends with the person we marry.

A wise man said:

There are friends who pretend to be friends,
but there is a friend who stays closer to you
than a brother or a sister. ***(Proverbs 18:24)***

Things that don't belong to us

viii. Thou shalt not steal.

8. LOVE YOUR NEIGHBOURS BY RESPECTING THEIR THINGS.

Stealing is taking things that don't belong to us.
It is one way of being selfish.
Wasting time, or being lazy, can be a way of stealing.
So can cheating people.
Just as we want people to be fair to us,
we ought to be fair to them.
We could even go further:
we could be generous with *our* things towards other people.

Jesus said:

If anyone wants to borrow, don't turn away.
(Matthew 5:42)

No telling tales

ix. Thou shalt not bear false witness against thy neighbour.

9. *LOVE YOUR NEIGHBOURS BY ALWAYS TELLING THE TRUTH.*

Telling the truth *to* them.
And the truth *about* them.
No telling tales.
We should be so honest and truthful
that people can always believe what we say.

St James said:

The tongue is a very small part of you,
but look how powerful it is.
It's like a little flame
that can set a whole forest alight.
It's like a wild animal
that no one has ever been able to tame. *(James 3:5-7)*

There's more to life than having things

x. Thou shalt not covet thy neighbour's goods.

10. LOVE YOUR NEIGHBOURS BY WISHING THEM WELL.

Wish them well with everything that is theirs.
Don't set your heart on what belongs to them.
We shouldn't be jealous of others.
Or greedy for ourselves.

Jesus said:

Don't be greedy.
There's more to life than having things. *(Luke 12:15)*

St Paul said:

Those who are greedy
are really worshipping another god. *(Ephesians 5:5)*

THIS IS HOW TO LIVE HAPPILY

1. Put God first, before anyone or anything else.
2. Realize that God is greater than any idea you have of him.
3. Use the word 'God' sparingly.
4. Remind yourself that God is with you every day.

5. Love your neighbours by respecting your parents.
6. Love your neighbours by never doing them any harm.
7. Love your neighbours by being faithful.
8. Love your neighbours by respecting their things.
9. Love your neighbours by always telling the truth.
10. Love your neighbours by wishing them well.

When someone asked Jesus which was the most important of the Commandments, he said:

Love God with all you've got,
and love your neighbour as carefully as you love yourself.
The whole Bible is based on this. *(Matthew 22:36-40)*